THIS POWERFUL RHYME
A Book of Sonnets

Edited by Helen Plotz

THOMAS Y. CROWELL CO.

The Earth Is the Lord's
Poems of the Spirit

Imagination's Other Place
Poems of Science and Mathematics

Poems from the German

Poems of Emily Dickinson

Poems of Robert Louis Stevenson

Untune the Sky
Poems of Music and the Dance

The Marvelous Light
Poets and Poetry

MACMILLAN PUBLISHING CO., INC.

The Pinnacled Tower
Selected Poems of Thomas Hardy

GREENWILLOW BOOKS

As I Walked Out One Evening
A Book of Ballads

The Gift Outright
America to Her Poets

Life Hungers to Abound
Poems of the Family

This Powerful Rhyme
A Book of Sonnets

THIS POWERFUL RHYME

A BOOK OF SONNETS

SELECTED BY HELEN PLOTZ

GREENWILLOW BOOKS
New York

To the memory of Milton
and to the many librarians in many cities
who have welcomed me

Pages 148–150 constitute
an extension of the copyright page.
"Sonneteering Made Easy" by S. B. Botsford reprinted
by permission; © 1962 The New Yorker Magazine, Inc.
Published by Greenwillow Books
A Division of William Morrow & Company, Inc.
105 Madison Avenue, New York, N.Y. 10016
Design by Ava Weiss
Printed in the United States of America
First Edition 10 9 8 7 6 5 4 3 2 1

Library of Congress Cataloging in Publication Data
Main entry under title: This powerful rhyme. Includes index.
Summary: Presents 130 sonnets from William Shakespeare,
John Donne, Richard Eberhart, Elizabeth Bishop, Edmund
Wilson, and others.
1. Sonnets, English. 2. Sonnets, American.
3. Children's poetry, English. 4. Children's poetry,
American. [1. Sonnets. 2. English poetry—Collections]
I. Plotz, Helen. PR1195.S5T4   821'.04   79-14037
ISBN 0-688-80226-5   ISBN 0-688-84226-7

Contents

Introduction

A powerful rhyme indeed. Since the word "sonnet"
entered our language in the sixteenth century, the
sonnet has survived innumerable fads and fancies as
well as more profound changes in the poetic tradition.
The rondeau and the triolet are dead—so is the epic.
I do not mean to imply that "Jenny kissed me,"
delightful as it is, is to be equated with "Paradise Lost,"
but simply to say that a contemporary poet would
neither play with one nor attempt the other.

The sonnet came to England from Italy, the land of
Dante and Petrarch. At first it followed the Petrarchan
model, that is, it consisted of an octave, or eight-line
stanza, followed by a sestet, or six-line stanza. The
Shakespearean sonnet, as it is now called, consists of
three four-line stanzas, followed by a rhyming couplet.
Both of these fourteen-line forms have been in
continuous use from Shakespeare's day to our own.
They are not, in this collection, segregated from each
other. It might be entertaining to think about whether
there is any other difference between them. Does
the period in which they were written determine the
form? Does the subject affect the form? I am simply
suggesting these questions. I do not know the answers,
nor, indeed, do I know whether there are any answers.

Most of us are familiar with Shakespeare and Wordsworth and Shelley and Keats as sonneteers. In selecting
the poems for this book I have deliberately left out
some of their most famous sonnets because I wished
to show a somewhat less familiar aspect of their

work. Ozymandias, King of Kings, is not here, but Buonaparte is.

The poems are divided into six sections. There is no rigid line between them. Many defy classification or could appear in more than one category.

I have chosen to begin with the sonnet itself. There are many poems, most but not all of them sonnets, about this difficult and fascinating invention.

The second category consists of sonnets of daily life in the city and in the country. Poems of Nature are here as well as poems about airplanes and subways.

The third section is devoted to Politics and to History, and the fourth to Religion and its many and often disturbing aspects.

Fifth are the poems of Love and Friendship and their opposites.

Last of all come the sonnets devoted to Time— our friend, our enemy, our rescuer, and our devourer.

Some believe that the rigid form of the sonnet has inhibited the free expression of emotion and the precision of thought which characterize great poetry. To those I can reply only that we who read these poems "have eyes to wonder, but lack tongues to praise."

Not marble, nor the gilded monuments
Of princes, shall outlive this pow'rful rhyme,
But you shall shine more bright in these contents
Than unswept stone, besmeared with sluttish time.
When wasteful war shall statues overturn,
And broils root out the work of masonry,
Nor Mars his sword nor war's quick fire shall burn
The living record of your memory.
'Gainst death and all oblivious enmity
Shall you pace forth; your praise shall still find room
Even in the eyes of all posterity
That wear this world out to the ending doom.
  So, till the judgment that yourself arise,
  You live in this, and dwell in lovers' eyes.

                       ∽ *William Shakespeare*

THE
SONNET

"So long as men can breathe,
or eyes can see"

Single Sonnet

Now, you great stanza, you heroic mould,
Bend to my will, for I must give you love:
The weight in the heart that breathes, but cannot move,
Which to endure flesh only makes so bold.

Take up, take up, as it were lead or gold
The burden; test the dreadful mass thereof.
No stone, slate, metal under or above
Earth, is so ponderous, so dull, so cold.

Too long as ocean bed bears up the ocean,
As earth's core bears the earth, have I borne this;
Too long have lovers, bending for their kiss,
Felt bitter force cohering without motion.

Staunch meter, great song, it is yours, at length,
To prove how stronger you are than my strength.

⌣ Louise Bogan

3

The Sonnet

(*Remembering Louise Bogan*)

The Sonnet, she told the crowd of bearded
    youths, their hands exploring
        rumpled girls,
        is a sacred

vessel: it takes a civilization
    to conceive its shape or know
        its uses. The kids
        stared as though

a Sphinx now spake the riddle of
    a blasted day. And few,
        she said, who would
        be *avant-garde*

consider that the term is drawn
    from tactics in the Prussian
        war, nor think
        when once they've breached

the fortress of a form, then send
        their shock troops yet again
          to breach the form,
          there's no form—

. . . they asked for her opinion of
       "the poetry of Rock."
        After a drink
        with the professors

she said, This is a bad time,
      bad, for poetry.
        Then with maenad
        gaze upon

the imaged ghost of a comelier day:
      I've enjoyed this visit,
        your wife's sheets
        are Irish linen.

                       ~ *Daniel Hoffman*

Memo to Góngora

To your language if not your native land,
Which is a tongue when all is said
That's done, perverse, gold, standard, and
Curiously conservative, as dead
As anything Amerigo invented,
I pilgrim with my accents in my hand
And your conceits unequalled in my head
Through volumes of rock and canticles of sand.
Like paradise, you are a promised land
Aflow with ilk and money, brine and wed-
lock, secrets that like circumstances stand
Unalterable, maps to be misread.
Were we translated here and now, instead
Of reading we might understand.

⌒ Daryl Hine

Luis de Góngora y Argote (1571–1627) was a Spanish
poet and contemporary of Shakespeare. An involved and
ornate style dominated his long poems; his sonnets were
simpler and more moving.—H.P.

To the Reader of These Sonnets

Into these loves who but for passion looks,
At this first sight here let him lay them by,
And seek elsewhere, in turning other books
Which better may his labor satisfy.
No farfetched sigh shall ever wound my breast,
Love from mine eye a tear shall never wring,
Nor in *Ah me's* my whining sonnets dressed.
A libertine, fantastically I sing;
My verse is the true image of my mind,
Ever in motion, still desiring change.
And as thus to variety inclined,
So in all humors sportively I range;
    My muse is rightly of the English strain,
    That cannot long one fashion entertain.

                         ～ *Michael Drayton*

On a Ruined House
in a Romantic Country

And this reft house is that the which he built,
Lamented Jack! And here his malt he pil'd,
Cautious in vain! These rats that squeak so wild,
Squeak, not unconscious of their father's guilt.
Did ye not see her gleaming through the glade?
Belike, 'twas she, the maiden all forlorn.
What though she milk no cow with crumpled horn,
Yet *ay* she haunts the dale where *erst* she stray'd;
And *ay* beside her stalks her amorous knight!
Still on his thighs their brogues are worn,
And through those brogues, still tatter'd and betorn,
His hindward charms gleam an unearthly white;
As when through broken clouds at night's high noon
Peeps in fair fragments forth the full-orb'd harvest-
    moon!

            ‿ *Samuel Taylor Coleridge*

This is one of several sonnets composed in humorous
imitation of the poets of Coleridge's day. It is a parody
of "The House That Jack Built."—H.P.

A Sonnet upon Sonnets

Fourteen, a sonneteer thy praises sings;
What magic myst'ries in that number lie!
Your hen hath fourteen eggs beneath her wings
That fourteen chickens to the roost may fly.
Fourteen full pounds the jockey's stone must be;
His age fourteen—a horse's prime is past.
Fourteen long hours too oft the Bard must fast;
Fourteen bright bumpers—bliss he ne'er must see!
Before fourteen, a dozen yields the strife;
Before fourteen—e'en thirteen's strength is vain.
Fourteen good years—a woman gives us life;
Fourteen good men—we lose that life again.
What lucubrations can be more upon it?
Fourteen good measur'd verses make a sonnet.

⌒ *Robert Burns*

To the Author of a Sonnet

Beginning " 'Sad is my verse,' you say, 'and yet no tear' "

Thy verse is "sad" enough, no doubt:
    A devilish deal more sad than witty!
Why we should weep I can't find out,
    Unless for *thee* we weep in pity.

Yet there is one I pity more;
    And much, alas! I think he needs it;
For he, I'm sure will suffer sore,
    Who, to his own misfortune, reads it.

Thy rhymes, without the aid of magic,
    May *once* be read—but never after:
Yet their effect's by no means tragic,
    Although by far too dull for laughter.

But would you make our bosoms bleed,
    And of no common pang complain—
If you would make us weep indeed,
    Tell us, you'll read them o'er again.

                   ∽ *George Gordon, Lord Byron*

Sonnet

He dreams of cheese that never feared a mouse—
    So mocked our poet of an elder day;
    And we who, idly dulcet, still essay
The palinode of these our *heres* and *nows,*
Whose palsied pulse may never more arouse
    The mounting sap that swells the buds of May—
    We scarce can tell the glimmer from the gray,
Nor, languid, loot September's laden boughs.

Ah, golden handmaids of Eurydice!
    Wild woodland satyrs at their wanton sport!
Great Homer's comrades!—I would rather be
    A beggar skulking the Piræan port
In sordid tatters, so I might but see
    Old lusty Triton rising with a snort!

⌒ Edmund Wilson

From "Memories of the Poetry of the Nineties, Written
Down While Waiting for Long-Distance Calls"

Sonnet

The master and the slave go hand in hand,
Though touch be lost. The poet is a slave,
And there be kings do sorrowfully crave
The joyance that a scullion may command.
But, ah, the sonnet-slave must understand
The mission of his bondage, or the grave
May clasp his bones, or ever he shall save
The perfect word that is the poet's wand.

The sonnet is a crown, whereof the rhymes
Are for Thought's purest gold the jewel-stones;
But shapes and echoes that are never done
Will haunt the workshop, as regret sometimes
Will bring with human yearning to sad thrones
The crash of battles that are never won.

∽ *Edwin Arlington Robinson*

Marble nor monuments whereof then we spoke
We speak of more; spasmodic as the wasp
About my windowpane, our short songs rasp—
Not those alone before their singers choke—
Our sweetest; none hopes now with one smart stroke
Or whittling years to crack away the hasp
Across the ticking future; all our grasp
Cannot beyond the butt secure its smoke.

A Renaissance fashion, not to be recalled.
We dinch "eternal numbers" and go out.
We understand exactly what we are.
. . . Do we? Argent I craft you as the star
Of flower-shut evening: who stays on to doubt
I sang true? ganger with trobador and scald!

〜 *John Berryman*

13

Sonneteering Made Easy

I

With hyphens, clip off endings that don't fit;
We call this "Hyper-Technic Line Expan-"
It has a certain rhythmic swing to it
That can't be got with ordinary scan-

Pentameter, iambic, is the rule
They teach in every other Sonnet School;
But we have found it simpler, if not nea-
To take occasional liberties with me-

Three quatrains and a couplet is the length
Of Shakespeare's sonnets, and of those by Mil-
It's standardized, like cheese from Brie or Stil-
The only difference being in the strength.

So now that we have settled length and ti-
Our Lesson Number II involves the rhy-

II

You'll note the scheme, "a," "b," "a," "b," above
In Quatrain One, that's perfectly O.K.
If something different's what you're thinking of,
See Quatrain Three, with its "a," "b," "b," "a."

For mittel quatrains we prefer to reck-
With what the Germans in their "schonnet" sprech
Employ: "a," "a," "b," "b;" ja, that's correct;
No German schonnet's e'er been besser sprecht.

So mix your "a"s and "b"s, your "b"s and "a"s
To suit your own convenience; any son-
Will have our professorial blessing on
If it is rhymed in one of these three ways.

The metre, length, and rhyme scheme now are def-
La porte est ouverte—simply put la clef.

III

The only item still to be discussed
Is subject matter, and we think you'll find
That Love is one that you can always trust
(Though Milton did quite well On Being Blind).

So Love it is, the simplest of all top-
Like "Frozen Love" or else "Love in the Trop-"
If you feel good, try "Love Is Here to Stay,"
And if you don't, there's "Love Has Gone Away."

Love's hot or cold; it moves like a thermom-
It's in, it's out, it's either up or down;
It's in the country or it stayed in town—
A Fair or Stormy, Wet or Dry barom-

So get a pencil and a piece of pa-
And you're all set to start "The Sonnet Ca-"

$\sim$ *S. B. Botsford*

Modified Sonnets

(Dedicated to adapters, abridgers, digesters,
and condensers everywhere)

SHALL I COMPARE THEE TO A SUMMER'S DAY?

Who says you're like one of the dog days?
You're nicer. And better.
Even in May, the weather can be gray,
And a summer sub-let doesn't last forever.
Sometimes the sun's too hot;
Sometimes it is not.
Who can stay young forever?
People break their necks or just drop dead!
But you? Never!
If there's just one condensed reader left
Who can figure out the abridged alphabet,
  After you're dead and gone,
  In this poem you'll live on!

MUSIC TO HEAR, WHY HEAR'ST THOU MUSIC SADLY?

Why are you listening to the radio, crying?
The program's good. You're nice. What could be
    wrong?
If you don't like it, why don't you try dialling?
Why keep humming if you don't like the song?
You're tuned in to the best jazz, rock, and classical
The unions make. If you don't like 'em,
Try, they're not bad, just a bit nonsensical.
Or maybe it's that you'd like to be alone? H'mmn?

16

Listen, it's as good as Kostelanetz!
You know what tone he gets out of the strings.
They sound like a happy family. Honest.
Like when the kids sing what the mother sings.
    There's a lesson in it, though. Hear that tone?
    One person couldn't do it. Don't live alone!!

WHEN IN DISGRACE WITH FORTUNE AND MEN'S EYES

When I'm out of cash and full of shame,
And crying to beat the band, alone,
And even God doesn't know my name,
And all I do is weep and moan,
I curse myself in the mirror,
Wishing I had a future,
Or some real pals, or was a good looker,
Or even a crazy artist or a deep thinker!
As I said, when even the old kicks seem tame,
And just when I hate myself the most,
I think about you. Then I'm o.k.
Just like a bird who hates the dirt
And can fly in the sky to get away.
    Thinking of you is as good as money.
    I'd give up royalties for you, honey.

$\sim$ *Howard Moss*

_____

These are three of Shakespeare's best-known sonnets.
—H.P.

Si Sic Omnia

As when *whenas* announced the formal sonnet,
Shoring eight lines against the noble six,
A pinched face peering from an old poke bonnet
Bespoke the rhymes of usual ready-mix.
Brave Baron Thought, the Reverend Moral Tone
Advanced upon pale reader hand in hand
And, finding his glass house without a stone,
Entered his cranium carefully trepanned.
Then, half aware of strange new-belfried bats
Promoting in their blind Petrarchan way
The dance of life, pale reader in new spats,
With polished crane, moved off to attend his day.
Klieg lights and kinescope may weave their spell,
But what it is old sonnets do not tell.

~David McCord

The Trapeze Performer

(For C. M.)

Fierce little bombs of gleam snap from his spangles,
Sleek flames glow softly on his silken tights,
The waiting crow blurs to crude darks and whites
Beneath the lamps that stare like savage bangles;
Safe in a smooth and sweeping arc he dangles
And sees the tanbark tower like old heights
Before careening eyes. At last he sights
The waiting hands and sinuously untangles.

Over the sheer abyss so deadly-near,
He falls, like wine to its appointed cup,
Turns like a wheel of fireworks, and is mine.
Battering hands acclaim our triumph clear.
—And steadfast muscles draw my sonnet up
To the firm iron of the fourteenth line.

$\sim$ *Stephen Vincent Benét*

19

Sonnet

This is the sonnet: fourteen lines for bones,
Sorrow for marrow, fleshed with life and death;
Small in the eye, biotic, out of breath,
Grey and mysterious in overtones.
Sunglass to Petrarch, a sonnet in the end
Held Milton's blindness, Shakespeare's tacit love,
Wordsworth's impinging world, Keats' star above
His loneliness. One was Rossetti's friend.
All things to all: first light, convective dark;
Young to the old, old magic to the young;
A cloud, a sail, a mountain, and a mark
Against the moon, the singer and the sung.
A stroller and a player, what is more,
Doubling in brass at Auden's marvelous Door.

∽ *David McCord*

Scorn not the Sonnet; Critic, you have frowned,
Mindless of its just honours; with this key
Shakspeare unlocked his heart; the melody
Of this small lute gave ease to Petrarch's wound;
A thousand times this pipe did Tasso sound;
With it Camöens soothed an exile's grief;
The Sonnet glittered a gay myrtle leaf
Amid the cypress with which Dante crowned
His visionary brow: a glow-worm lamp,
It cheered mild Spenser, called from Faery-land
To struggle through dark ways; and, when a damp
Fell round the path of Milton, in his hand
The Thing became a trumpet; whence he blew
Soul-animating strains—alas, too few!

⌒ *William Wordsworth*

Robert Browning said of this sonnet: ". . . 'with this
same key/Shakespeare unlocked his heart,' once more!"
Did Shakespeare? If so, the less Shakespeare he!—H.P.

The Sonnet

A sonnet is a moment's monument—
Memorial from the Soul's eternity
To one dead deathless hour. Look that it be,
Whether for lustral rite or dire portent,
Of its own arduous fullness reverent,
Carve it in ivory or in ebony,
As Day or Night may rule; and let Time see
Its flowering crest impearled and orient.
A sonnet is a coin; its face reveals
The Soul—its converse, to what Power 'tis due:—
Whether for tribute to the august appeals
Of life, or dower in Love's high retinue,
It serve; or 'mid the dark wharf's cavernous breath,
In Charon's palm it pay the toll to Death.

⌒ *Dante Gabriel Rossetti*

DAILY LIFE

"These present days"

Happy the Man

Happy the man who, journeying far and wide
As Jason or Ulysses did, can then
Turn homeward, seasoned in the ways of men,
And claim his own, and there in peace abide!

When shall I see the chimney-smoke divide
The sky above my little town: ah, when
Stroll the small gardens of that house again
Which is my realm and crown, and more beside?

Better I love the plain, secluded home
My fathers built, than bold façades of Rome;
Slate pleases me as marble cannot do;

Better than Tiber's flood the quiet Loire.
Those little hills than these, and dearer far
Than great sea winds the zephyrs of Anjou.

$\sim$ *Richard Wilbur*

Happy is England! I could be content
   To see no other verdure than its own,
   To feel no other breezes than are blown
Through its tall woods with high romances blent.
Yet do I sometimes feel a languishment
   For skies Italian, and an inward groan
   To sit upon an Alp as on a throne,
And half forget what world or worldling meant.
Happy is England, sweet her artless daughters,
   Enough their simple loveliness for me,
     Enough their whitest arms in silence clinging.
   Yet do I often warmly burn to see
     Beauties of deeper glance, and hear their singing,
And float with them about the summer waters.

               ∽ *John Keats*

Alexander Calder

When one leaf, left hanging on a bough
Pruned sharply by the quickness of the frost,
Fluttering, turns sideways and is lost,
The watcher's eye is opened and sees, now
One shape becoming many as it moves.
In arranged patterns the slow planets turn
But do not alter, so that the eye can learn
Movement controlled in unseen grooves.

Here leaf and planet can combine
To shift upon their slender wires,
Can circle, searching for a line
Or soar around sharp metal spires.

These captive stars are docile and obey
Their maker's whims of change and interplay.

〜 *Ruthven Todd*

Good Humor Man

Listen! It is the summer's self that ambles
   Through the green lanes with such a coaxing tongue.
Not birds or daisy fields were ever symbols
   More proper to the time than this bell rung
With casual insistence—no, not swallow
   Circling the roof or bee in hollyhock.
His is the season's voice, and children follow,
   Panting, from every doorway down the block.

So, long ago, in some such shrill procession
   Perhaps the Hamelin children gave pursuit
To one who wore a red-and-yellow fashion
   Instead of white, but made upon his flute
The selfsame promise plain to every comer:
Unending sweets, imperishable summer.

                       Phyllis McGinley

The Subway

Dark accurate plunger down the successive knell
Of arch on arch, where ogives burst a red
Reverberance of hail upon the dead
Thunder like an exploding crucible!
Harshly articulate, musical steel shell
Of angry worship, hurled religiously
Upon your business of humility
Into the iron forestries of hell:

Till broken in the shift of quieter
Dense altitudes tangential of your steel,
I am become geometries, and glut
Expansions like a blind astronomer
Dazed, while the worldless heavens bulge and reel
In the cold revery of an idiot.

$\sim$ *Allen Tate*

On the Grasshopper and Cricket

The poetry of earth is never dead:
  When all the birds are faint with the hot sun,
  And hide in cooling trees, a voice will run
From hedge to hedge about the new-mown mead;
That is the Grasshopper's—he takes the lead
  In summer luxury,—he has never done
  With his delights; for when tired out with fun
He rests at ease beneath some pleasant weed.
The poetry of earth is ceasing never:
  On a lone winter evening, when the frost
    Has wrought a silence, from the stove there shrills
The Cricket's song, in warmth increasing ever,
  And seems to one in drowsiness half lost,
    The Grasshopper's among some grassy hills.

⌒ John Keats

Night Flight, over Ocean

Sweet fish tinned in the innocence of sleep,
we passengers parallel navigate
the firmament's subconscious-colored deep,
streaming aligned toward a landlocked gate.
Schooled (in customs, in foreign coin), from zone
to zone we slip, each clutching at the prize
(a camera, a seduction) torn from some lone
shore lost in our brain like the backs of our eyes.
Nationless, nowhere, we dream the ocean
we motionless plummet above, our roaring
discreet as a stewardess padding, stray yen
or shillings jingling in the sky of our snoring.
Incipient, we stir; we burgeon, blank
dim swimmers borne toward the touchdown spank.

⌒ *John Updike*

Aerial

Inaccurately from an old rocking chair
One saw the rivery lands and lifted snows.
Then the Wrights' fabrication and Blériot's
Annexed the cumulus kingdom of the air.
Helmeted birdmen looped the loop at the Fair
And ranged in later squadrons to impose
On somber towns the tremor of their blows
Or lightning stitches, adding flare on flare.
So much of heaven gained, so much of hell,
Made way for transcendental craft ensuing,
Emissaries not to be disavowed;
But let us pause on thee, sweet Caravel,
Dauphin of jets, in azure halls reviewing
Tall *parfaits* and pudding of whipped cloud.

∽ *Robert Fitzgerald*

To a Goose

If thou didst feed on western plains of yore;
Or waddle wide with flat and flabby feet
Over some Cambrian mountain's plashy moor;
Or find in farmer's yard a safe retreat
From gipsy thieves, and foxes sly and fleet;
If thy grey quills, by lawyer guided, trace
Deeds big with ruin to some wretched race,
Or love-sick poet's sonnet, sad and sweet,
Wailing the rigour of his lady fair;
Or if, the drudge of housemaid's daily toil,
Cobwebs and dust thy pinions white besoil,
Departed Goose! I neither know nor care.
But this I know, that we pronounced thee fine,
Season'd with sage and onions, and port wine.

～ *Robert Southey*

The Foddering Boy

The foddering boy along the crumping snows
With straw-band-belted legs and folded arm
Hastens, and on the blast that keenly blows
Oft turns for breath, and beats his fingers warm,
And shakes the lodging snows from off his clothes,
Buttoning his doublet closer from the storm
And slouching his brown beaver o'er his nose—
Then faces it agen, and seeks the stack
Within its circling fence where hungry lows
Expecting cattle, making many a track
About the snow, impatient for the sound
When in huge forkfuls trailing at his back
He litters the sweet hay about the ground
And brawls to call the staring cattle round.

~ *John Clare*

Schoolboys in Winter

The schoolboys still their morning rambles take
To neighbouring village school with playing speed,
Loitering with pastime's leisure till they quake,
Oft looking up the wild-geese droves to heed,
Watching the letters which their journeys make;
Or plucking haws on which the fieldfares feed,
And hips, and sloes; and on each shallow lake
Making glib slides, where they like shadows go
Till some fresh pastimes in their minds awake.
Then off they start anew and hasty blow
Their numbed and clumpsing fingers till they glow;
Then races with their shadows wildly run
That stride huge giants o'er the shining snow
In the pale splendour of the winter sun.

~ *John Clare*

Fresh Spring, the herald of love's mighty king,
    In whose coat armour richly are displayed
All sorts of flowers the which on earth do spring
    In goodly colours gloriously arrayed;
    Go to my love, where she is careless laid,
Yet in her winter's bower not well awake;
    Tell her the joyous time will not be stayed
Unless she do him by the forelock take.
Bid her therefore herself soon ready make,
    To wait on Love amongst his lovely crew;
Where every one that misseth then her make
    Shall be by him amerced with penance due.
        Make haste therefore, sweet love, whilst it is prime
        For none can call again the passed time.

⤳ *Edmund Spenser*

Spring

Nothing is so beautiful as spring—
    When weeds, in wheels, shoot long and lovely
        and lush;
    Thrush's eggs look little low heavens, and thrush
Through the echoing timber does so rinse and wring
The ear, it strikes like lightnings to hear him sing;
    The glassy peartree leaves and blooms, they brush
    The descending blue; that blue is all in a rush
With richness; the racing lambs too have fair their fling.

What is all this juice and all this joy?
    A strain of the earth's sweet being in the beginning
In Eden garden.—Have, get, before it cloy,
    Before it cloud, Christ, lord, and sour with sinning,
Innocent mind and Mayday in girl and boy,
    Most, O maid's child, thy choice and worthy the
        winning.

                    ~ *Gerard Manley Hopkins*

Sonnet

The winter deepening, the hay all in,
The barn fat with cattle, the apple-crop
Conveyed to market or the fragrant bin,
He thinks the time has come to make a stop,

And sinks half-grudging in his firelit seat,
Though with his heavy body's full consent,
In what would be the posture of defeat,
But for that look of rigorous content.

Outside, the night dives down like one great crow
Against his cast-off clothing where it stands
Up to the knees in miles of hustled snow,

Flapping and jumping like a kind of fire,
And floating skyward its abandoned hands
In gestures of invincible desire.

～ *Richard Wilbur*

Admonitions to a Lovely Winter Morning

What coquetry just cockcrow past first light—
To sprinkle diamonds in your unkempt hair
To blank the lingering traces of the night—
Squandered snowdust settling everywhere.
What vanity! to atomize such spumes
Of paralysing scent that everything
About is soused in frost-distilled perfumes
Benumbing very memory of Spring.
Look to the chores! Come feed the chickadees,
Set sluggish streams to scrub their stony faces,
Send chipmunks marketing among the trees,
Release us from the grip of your embraces
Lest frozen we neglect our workday duty
In truant admiration of your beauty.

⁓ Raymond Henri

August Nostalgia

This is the first of August when, at home,
The first warm smell of apples roughs the air
And crowding weeds have drunk a richened flair
For gorgeousness from field soil mixed with chrome.
Purple and pink! No ordinary loam
Could make such waves of color break and bear
Their vivid seaware up the land to where
The brook leaves flowers as a ship leaves foam
Along its curving wake. Purple and gold—
And frail, black-centered white of Queen Anne's Lace.
The earth goes home to August every year
And has those satisfying fields to hold
In hungry arms and press against her face.
. . . But I can smell the apples even here.

$\sim$ *Louise Townsend Nicholl*

Season of change the sun for distaff bearing
In your right hand and in the left large rains
And writhen winds and noiselessly forth faring
The earth abroad, and streaming wide your skeins,
When in unfathomed fairness you have clothed
The sea with quiet, the land with painless wealth,
Turn you to those who changelessly have loathed
All and their kind, and grant them peace and health:
The proud stone-parting ardor of the tree,
The glee of ice relaxed against new earth,
Joy of the lamb and lust of bloom-struck bee
Grant to the sick, stiff, spiteful, like fresh birth.
Let this new time no natural wheel derange:
Be ever changeless, thus: season of change.

＾ *James Agee*

The Hawk

The brazen-footed hawk above the wood
Banks silently, and silently the sun
Tips beak and claw as with that creature's blood
Whose day was done before this day was done.

As he the ground, so we scan heaven for change—
Hawk's-eyed, yet groundlings chiefly—one with those
Who wait the stranger known as worse than strange:
A sudden air-borne shadow skimming close
To merge impossible fantasy with fact,
To rend surprise in two and hold the prize
Before reaction can defeat the act
Or premonition show monition wise.

Here, bloodied only by the sun, we stay
In waiting for what does not come, but may.

                                        ∾ *Carlos Baker*

Praise in Summer

Obscurely yet most surely called to praise,
As sometimes summer calls us all, I said
The hills are heavens full of branching ways
Where star-nosed moles fly overhead the dead;
I said the trees are mines in air, I said
See how the sparrow burrows in the sky!
And then I wondered why this mad *instead*
Perverts our praise to uncreation, why
Such savor's in this wrenching things awry.
Does sense so stale that it must needs derange
The world to know it? To a praiseful eye
Should it not be enough of fresh and strange
That trees grow green, and moles can course in clay,
And sparrows sweep the ceiling of our day?

$\sim$ *Richard Wilbur*

43

Sonnet on Rare Animals

Like deer *rat-tat* before we reach the clearing
I frighten what I brought you out to see,
Telling you who are tired by now of hearing
How there are five, how they take no fright of me.
I tried to point out fins inside the reef
Where the coral reef had turned the water dark;
The bathers kept the beach in half-belief
But would not swim and could not see the shark.
I have alarmed on your behalf and others'
Sauntering things galore.
It is this way with verse and animals
And love, that when you point you lose them all.
Startled or on a signal, what is rare
Is off before you have it anywhere.

~ *William Meredith*

Burden

Whoever lives beside a mountain knows,
Although he dares not speak it out, that he
Must always carry on his heart the snows
That burden down the trees. And never the sea
Will rush around him cool, like snow-cool air,
And carry him and lift him like a leaf.
He will not find this lightness anywhere
Since mountains brood, they hold dark league
      with grief.

The pine trees never tire of moving down
The slopes to meet him, pointing up from town
Beyond the tree-line to the rigid peaks.
The mountain holds him though it never speaks.
He scrambles over boulders on his knees
Trying to reach the summit, like the trees.

                ~ *Richard Eberhart*

Some Dreams They Forgot

The dead birds fell, but no one had seen them fly,
or could guess from where. They were black, their eyes
    were shut,
and no one knew what kind of birds they were. But
all held them and looked up through the new far-
    funneled sky.
Also, dark drops fell. Night-collected on the eaves,
or congregated on the ceilings over their beds,
they hung, mysterious drop-shapes, all night over their
    heads,
now rolling off their careless fingers quick as dew off
    leaves.
Where had they seen wood-berries perfect black as these,
shining just so in early morning? Dark-hearted decoys on
upper-bough or below-leaf. Had they thought *poison*
and left? or—remember—eaten them from the loaded
    trees?
What flowers shrink to seeds like these, like columbine?
But their dreams are all inscrutable by eight or nine.

                   ⌢ Elizabeth Bishop

POLITICS AND HISTORY

"The child of state"

Sonnet on Chillon

Eternal Spirit of the chainless Mind!
  Brightest in dungeons, Liberty! thou art,
  For there thy habitation is the heart—
The heart which love of thee alone can bind;
And when thy sons to fetters are consigned—
  To fetters, and the damp vault's dayless gloom,
  Their country conquers with their martyrdom,
And Freedom's fame finds wings on every wind.
Chillon! thy prison is a holy place,
  And thy sad floor an altar—for 'twas trod,
Until his very steps have left a trace
  Worn, as if thy cold pavement were a sod,
By Bonnivard!—May none those marks efface!
  For they appeal from tyranny to God.

∽ George Gordon, Lord Byron

François de Bonnivard (1493–1570) was a Swiss patriot
imprisoned by the Duke of Savoy on the island of
Chillon in Lake Geneva.—H.P.

Anthem for Doomed Youth

What passing-bells for these who die as cattle?
   Only the monstrous anger of the guns.
   Only the stuttering rifles' rapid rattle
Can patter out their hasty orisons.
No mockeries now for them; no prayers nor bells,
   Nor any voice of mourning save the choirs,—
The shrill, demented choirs of wailing shells;
   And bugles calling for them from sad shires.

What candles may be held to speed them all?
   Not in the hands of boys, but in their eyes
Shall shine the holy glimmers of good-byes.
   The pallor of girls' brows shall be their pall;
Their flowers the tenderness of patient minds.
And each slow dusk a drawing-down of blinds.

                 ~ *Wilfred Owen*

A Soldier

He is that fallen lance that lies as hurled,
That lies unlifted now, come dew, come rust,
But still lies pointed as it plowed the dust.
If we who sight along it round the world,
See nothing worthy to have been its mark,
It is because like men we look too near,
Forgetting that as fitted to the sphere,
Our missiles always make too short an arc.
They fall, they rip the grass, they intersect
The curve of earth, and striking, break their own;
They make us cringe for metal-point on stone.
But this we know, the obstacle that checked
And tripped the body, shot the spirit on
Further than target ever showed or shone.

～ *Robert Frost*

The Old Bridge at Florence

Taddeo Gaddi built me. I am old,
　　Five centuries old. I plant my foot of stone
　　Upon the Arno, as St. Michael's own
　　Was planted on the dragon. Fold by fold
Beneath me as it struggles, I behold
　　Its glistening scales. Twice hath it overthrown
　　My kindred and companions. Me alone
　　It moveth not, but is by me controlled.
I can remember when the Medici
　　Were driven from Florence; longer still ago
　　The final wars of Ghibelline and Guelf.
Florence adorns me with her jewelry;
　　And when I think that Michael Angelo
　　Hath leaned on me, I glory in myself.

　　　　　⁓ Henry Wadsworth Longfellow

On the Extinction
of the Venetian Republic

Once did She hold the gorgeous East in fee,
And was the safeguard of the West; the worth
Of Venice did not fall below her birth,
Venice, the eldest child of liberty.
She was a maiden city, bright and free;
No guile seduced, no force could violate;
And, when she took unto herself a mate,
She must espouse the everlasting Sea.
And what if she had seen those glories fade,
Those titles vanish, and that strength decay;
Yet shall some tribute of regret be paid
When her long life hath reached its final day:
Men are we, and must grieve when even the shade
Of that which once was great, is passed away.

∽ *William Wordsworth*

Napoleon conquered the republic of Venice and gave
the city to Austria in 1797. In the next seventeen years,
the control of Venice shuttled back and forth
between France and Austria. This sonnet was written
in 1802.—H.P.

Cyriack, whose Grandsire on the Royal Bench
    Of British *Themis*, with no mean applause
    Pronounc't and in his volumes taught our Laws,
    Which others at their Bar so often wrench;
Today deep thoughts resolve with me to drench
    In mirth, that after no repenting draws;
    Let *Euclid* rest and *Archimedes* pause,
    And what the *Swede* intend, and what the *French*.
To measure life, learn thou betimes, and know
    Toward solid good what leads the nearest way;
    For other things mild Heav'n a time ordains,
And disapproves that care, though wise in show,
    That with superfluous burden loads the day,
    And when God sends a cheerful hour, refrains.

                     ∽ *John Milton*

Cyriack Skinner's grandfather was Sir Edward Coke,
Lord Chief Justice of England, and a staunch upholder
of the common law.—H.P.

To Mr. Cyriack Skinner upon His Blindness

Cyriack, this three years' day these eyes, though clear
    To outward view, of blemish or of spot;
    Bereft of light their seeing have forgot,
    Nor to their idle orbs doth sight appear
Of Sun or Moon or Star throughout the year,
    Or man or woman. Yet I argue not
    Against heaven's hand or will, nor bate a jot
    Of heart or hope; but still bear up and steer
Right onward. What supports me, dost thou ask?
    The conscience, Friend, to have lost them overply'd
    In liberty's defence, my noble task,
Of which all Europe talks from side to side.
    This thought might lead me through the
      world's vain mask
    Content though blind, had I no better guide.

                 ∿ *John Milton*

To Toussaint L'Ouverture

Toussaint, the most unhappy man of men!
Whether the whistling Rustic tend his plough
Within thy hearing, or thy head be now
Pillowed in some deep dungeon's earless den;—
O miserable Chieftain! where and when
Wilt thou find patience! Yet die not; do thou
Wear rather in thy bonds a cheerful brow:
Though fallen thyself, never to rise again,
Live, and take comfort. Thou hast left behind
Powers that will work for thee; air, earth, and skies;
There's not a breathing of the common wind
That will forget thee; thou hast great allies;
Thy friends are exultations, agonies,
And love, and man's unconquerable mind.

$\sim$ *William Wordsworth*

François Dominique Toussaint L'Ouverture (1743–1803)
was a black general and the liberator of the island of
Haiti.—H.P.

Black Majesty

(After reading John W. Vandercook's chronicle of sable glory)

These men were kings, albeit they were black,
Christophe and Dessalines and L'Ouverture;
Their majesty has made me turn my back
Upon a plaint I once shaped to endure.
These men were black, I say, but they were crowned
And purple-clad, however brief their time.
Stifle your agony; let grief be drowned;
We know joy had a day once and a clime.

Dark gutter-snipe, black sprawler-in-the-mud,
A thing men did a man may do again.
What answer filters through your sluggish blood
To these dark ghosts who knew so bright a reign?
"Lo, I am dark, but comely," Sheba sings.
"And we were black," three shades reply, "but kings."

～ Countee Cullen

Henri Christophe (1767–1820) and Jean Jacques
Dessalines (1758–1806) were black kings of Haiti.—H.P.

A Sonnet

Addressed to Mr. Phillips Printer now in confinement
at Leicester

Phillips! the suff'rer less by law than pow'r,
   Though prison'd in an adamantine hold,
   May bear a heart as free and uncontroul'd
In his dark cell, as in a summer's bow'r.

The sly accuser—He, who in an hour
   When all suspicion slept like Him of old
   Eve's Tempter, wreath'd in many an artful fold
Conceal'd his drift with purpose to devour—

He is the pris'ner, and those ribs within
   That hoop his sorry vitals round about
Dwells one, who never shall compassion win
   Feel what he may, 'till Judgment call him out.

Thou then less deeply at thy wrongs repine,
Scorn is his meed, commiseration thine.

                    ~ *William Cowper*

Mr. Phillips was imprisoned because he sold Thomas
Paine's *Rights of Man* in his bookshop.—H.P.

A Misunderstanding

Just as his dream foretold, he met them all:
The smiling grimy boy at the garage
Ran out before he blew his horn; the tall
Professor in the mountains with his large
Tweed pockets full of plants addressed him hours
Before he would have dared; the deaf girl too
Seemed to expect him at her green chateau;
A meal was laid, the guest-room full of flowers.

More, their talk always took the wished-for turn,
Dwelt on the need for someone to advise,
Yet, at each meeting, he was forced to learn
The same misunderstanding would arise.
Which was in need of help? Were they or he
The physician, bridegroom and incendiary?

 ～ *W. H. Auden*

Hope Is Not for the Wise

Hope is not for the wise, fear is for fools;
Change and the world, we think, are racing to a fall,
Open-eyed and helpless, in every newscast
    that is the news:
The time's events would seem mere chaos but all
Drift the one deadly direction. But this is only
The August thunder of the age, not the November.
Wise men hope nothing, the wise are naturally lonely
And think November as good as April,
    the wise remember
That Caesar and even final Augustulus had heirs,
And men lived on; rich unplanned life on earth
After the foreign wars and the civil wars,
    the border wars
And the barbarians: music and religion,
    honor and mirth
Renewed life's lost enchantments. But if life even
Had perished utterly, Oh perfect loveliness
    of earth and heaven.

〜 Robinson Jeffers

If We Must Die

If we must die, let it not be like hogs
Hunted and penned in an inglorious spot,
While round us bark the mad and hungry dogs,
Making their mock at our accursed lot.
If we must die, O let us nobly die,
So that our precious blood may not be shed
In vain; then even the monsters we defy
Shall be constrained to honor us though dead!
O kinsmen! we must meet the common foe!
Though far outnumbered let us show us brave,
And for their thousand blows deal one deathblow!
What though before us lies the open grave?
Like men we'll face the murderous, cowardly pack,
Pressed to the wall, dying, but fighting back!

～ *Claude McKay*

On the Death
of Senator Thomas J. Walsh

An old man more is gathered to the great.
    Singly, for conscience' sake he bent his brow:
He served that mathematic thing, the State,
    And with the great will be forgotten now.
The State is voiceless: only, we may write
    Singly our thanks for service past, and praise
The man whose purpose and remorseless sight
    Pursued corruption for its evil ways.

How sleep the great, the gentle, and the wise!
    Agëd and calm, they couch the wrinkled head.
Done with the wisdom that mankind devise,
    Humbly they render back the volume read—
Dwellers amid a peace that few surmise,
    Masters of quiet among all the dead.

∾ Yvor Winters

Thomas J. Walsh (1859–1933), senator from Montana,
was a fighter for women's suffrage and for the abolition
of child labor.—H.P.

Salem

In Salem seasick spindrift drifts or skips
To the canvas flapping on the seaward panes
Until the knitting sailor stabs at ships
Nosing like sheep of Morpheus through his brain's
Asylum. Seaman, seaman, how the draft
Lashes the oily slick about your head,
Beating up whitecaps! Seaman, Charon's raft
Dumps its damned goods into the harbor-bed,—
There sewage sickens the rebellious seas.
Remember, seaman, Salem fishermen
Once hung their nimble fleets on the Great Banks.
Where was it that New England bred the men
Who quartered the Leviathan's fat flanks
And fought the British Lion to his knees?

～ *Robert Lowell*

Who's Who

A shilling life will give you all the facts:
How Father beat him, how he ran away,
What were the struggles of his youth, what acts
Made him the greatest figure of his day:
Of how he fought, fished, hunted, worked all night,
Though giddy, climbed new mountains; named a sea:
Some of the last researchers even write
Love made him weep his pints like you and me.

With all his honours on, he sighed for one
Who, say astonished critics, lived at home;
Did little jobs about the house with skill
And nothing else; could whistle; would sit still
Or potter round the garden; answered some
Of his long marvellous letters but kept none.

∽ *W. H. Auden*

To Inez Milholland

*Read in Washington, November eighteenth, 1923,
at the unveiling of a statue of three leaders in the
cause of Equal Rights for Women*

Upon this marble bust that is not I
Lay the round, formal wreath that is not fame;
But in the forum of my silenced cry
Root ye the living tree whose sap is flame.
I, that was proud and valiant, am no more;—
Save as a dream that wanders wide and late,
Save as a wind that rattles the stout door,
Troubling the ashes in the sheltered grate.
The stone will perish; I shall be twice dust.
Only my standard on a taken hill
Can cheat the mildew and the red-brown rust
And make immortal my adventurous will.
Even now the silk is tugging at the staff:
Take up the song; forget the epitaph.

❧ *Edna St. Vincent Millay*

Inez Milholland (1886–1916) was an impassioned fighter
for women's rights.—H.P.

Feelings of a Republican on the Fall of Bonaparte

I hated thee, fallen tyrant; I did groan
To think that a most unambitious slave,
Like thou, shouldst dance and revel on the grave
Of Liberty. Thou mightst have built thy throne
Where it had stood even now: thou didst prefer
A frail and bloody pomp which Time has swept
In fragments towards Oblivion. Massacre,
For this I prayed, would on thy sleep have crept,
Treason and Slavery, Rapine, Fear, and Lust,
And stifled thee, their minister. I know
Too late, since thou and France are in the dust,
That Virtue owns a more eternal foe
Than Force or Fraud: old Custom, legal Crime,
And bloody Faith the foulest birth of Time.

$\sim$ *Percy Bysshe Shelley*

To Kosciusko

Good Kosciusko, thy great name alone
  Is a full harvest whence to reap high feeling;
  It comes upon us like the glorious pealing
Of the wide spheres—an everlasting tone.
And now it tells me that in worlds unknown
  The names of heroes burst from clouds concealing
  And change to harmonies, for ever stealing
Through cloudless blue and round each silver throne.
It tells me too, that on a happy day,
  When some good spirit walks upon the earth,
    Thy name, with Alfred's and the great of yore
  Gently commingling, gives tremendous birth
To a loud hymn, that sounds far, far away
    To where the great God lives for evermore.

∽ John Keats

Tadeus Kosciusko (1746–1817), a volunteer in
Washington's army, was awarded American citizenship in
gratitude for his devotion to the cause of American
independence. On his return to Poland, he fought valiantly
but unsuccessfully for Polish independence. Like his
contemporaries Jefferson and Lafayette, he believed in
liberty and equality under the law.—H.P.

Poland

How long, O God, shall men be ridden down,
And trampled under by the last and least
Of men? The heart of Poland hath not ceased
To quiver, tho' her sacred blood doth drown
The fields, and out of every smouldering town
Cries to Thee, lest brute Power be increased,
Till that o'ergrown Barbarian in the East
Transgress his ample bound to some new crown:—
Cries to Thee, "Lord, how long shall these things be?
How long this icy-hearted Muscovite
Oppress the region?" Us, O Just and Good,
Forgive, who smiled when she was torn in three;
Us, who stand now, when we should aid the right—
A matter to be wept with tears of blood!

～ *Alfred, Lord Tennyson*

Why I Am a Liberal

"Why?" Because all I haply can and do,
　　All that I am now, all I hope to be,—
　　Whence comes it save from fortune setting free
Body and soul the purpose to pursue
God traced for both? If fetters, not a few,
　　Of prejudice, convention, fall from me,
　　These shall I bid men—each in his degree
Also God-guided—bear, and gaily too?

But little do or can the best of us:
　　That little is achieved through Liberty.
Who then dares hold—emancipated thus—
　　His fellow shall continue bound? Not I,
Who live, love, labour freely, nor discuss
　　A brother's right to freedom. That is "Why."

　　　　　　　　　⁓ Robert Browning

Sonnet: Political Greatness

Nor happiness, nor majesty, nor fame,
Nor peace, nor strength, nor skill in arms or arts,
Shepherd those herds whom tyranny makes tame;
Verse echoes not one beating of their hearts,
History is but the shadow of their shame,
Art veils her glass, or from the pageant starts
As to oblivion their blind millions fleet,
Staining that Heaven with obscene imagery
Of their own likeness. What are numbers knit
By force or custom? Man who man would be,
Must rule the empire of himself; in it
Must be supreme, establishing his throne
On vanquished will, quelling the anarchy
Of hopes and fears, being himself alone.

⌒ Percy Bysshe Shelley

RELIGION

*"The center of my
sinful earth"*

Poor soul, the center of my sinful earth,
My sinful earth these rebel pow'rs that thee array,
Why dost thou pine within and suffer dearth,
Painting thy outward walls so costly gay?
Why so large cost, having so short a lease,
Dost thou upon thy fading mansion spend?
Shall worms, inheritors of this excess,
Eat up thy charge? Is this thy body's end?
Then, soul, live thou upon thy servant's loss,
And let that pine to aggravate thy store;
Buy terms divine in selling hours of dross;
Within be fed, without be rich no more:
    So shalt thou feed on Death, that feeds on men,
    And Death once dead, there's no more dying then.

$\sim$ *William Shakespeare*

To the Lord General Cromwell, on the Proposals of Certain Ministers at the Committee for Propagation of the Gospel

Cromwell, our chief of men, who through a cloud
   Not of war only, but detractions rude,
   Guided by faith and matchless fortitude,
   To peace and truth thy glorious way hast ploughed,
And on the neck of crownèd Fortune proud
   Hast reared God's trophies, and his work pursued,
   While Darwen stream, with blood of Scots imbrued,
   And Dunbar field, resounds thy praises loud,
And Worcester's laureate wreath: yet much remains
   To conquer still; Peace hath her victories
   No less renowned than War: new foes arise,
Threatening to bind our souls with secular chains.
   Help us to save free conscience from the paw
   Of hireling wolves, whose Gospel is their maw.

∽ John Milton

The Genuine Article

You do not love the Bourgeoisie. Of course: for they
Begot you, bore you, paid for you, and punched
    your head;
You work with them; they're intimate as board and bed;
How could you love them, meeting them thus every day?
You love the Proletariat, the thin, far-away
Abstraction which resembles any workman fed
On mortal food as closely as the shiny red
Chessknight resembles stallions when they
    stamp and neigh.

For kicks are dangerous; riding schools are painful,
    coarse
And ribald places. Every way it costs far less
To learn the harmless manage of the wooden horse
—So calculably taking the small jumps of chess.
Who, that can love nonentities, would choose the labour
Of loving the quotidian face and fact, his neighbour?

             ~ *C. S. Lewis*

Jeremiah:

Roses have been his bed so long that he
Constructs a mat of thorns for lying on;
People have flattered him, until the sea
Becomes a preferable monotone.
He sets his masonry upon the brink
Of lamentation, out of his window peers
Toward waves that ever rise only to sink
Confused and lost as he among his years.
A ship alive becomes to him a hull
Charred and undone, the fumble of a wreck;
His dreams are but the droppings of a gull
Caught in a noose of seaweed round his neck;
And crying like a maniac toward the sky,
He pulls mankind in after him, to die.

～ *Witter Bynner*

Light of this world, whom the world tries to darken,
Lord of this world, whom faith alone can find,
Word of this world, to whom men will not hearken,
Bright presence to whose radiance men are blind,
View with compassion your revolving wheel,
That primal gift, now whirling to destruction;
Your gold converted to a blast of steel,
Your wisdom twisted by adroit corruption.
In lonely spirits here and there inflame
Austere enthusiasm for the plan
When in your image first, and then your name,
Would have created the triumphant Man.
Speak immortality through them, wage war
On Things men worship, that men live once more.

∽ *Robert Hillyer*

Acceptance

When the spent sun throws up its rays on cloud
And goes down burning into the gulf below,
No voice in nature is heard to cry aloud
At what has happened. Birds, at least, must know
It is the change to darkness in the sky.
Murmuring something quiet in her breast,
One bird begins to close a faded eye;
Or overtaken too far from his nest,
Hurrying low above the grove, some waif
Swoops just in time to his remembered tree.
At most he thinks or twitters softly, "Safe!
Now let the night be dark for all of me.
Let the night be too dark for me to see
Into the future. Let what will be, be."

∾ Robert Frost

The Starlight Night

Look at the stars! look, look up at the skies!
  O look at all the fire-folk sitting in the air!
  The bright boroughs, the circle-citadels there!
Down in dim woods the diamond delves! the elves'-eyes!
The grey lawns cold where gold, where quickgold lies!
  Wind-beat whitebeam! airy abeles set on a flare!
  Flake-doves sent floating forth at a farmyard scare!—
Ah well! it is all a purchase, all is a prize.

Buy then! bid then!—What?—Prayer, patience, alms,
  vows.
Look, look: a May-mess, like on orchard boughs!
  Look! March-bloom, like on mealed-with-yellow
    sallows!
These are indeed the barn; withindoors house
The shocks. This piece-bright paling shuts the spouse
  Christ home, Christ and his mother and all his
    hallows.

       ∼ Gerard Manley Hopkins

Redemption

Having been tenant long to a rich Lord,
   Not thriving, I resolved to be bold,
   And make a suit unto him to afford
A new small-rented lease and cancel th' old.
In heaven at his manor I him sought.
   They told me there that he was lately gone
   About some land which he had dearly bought
Long since on earth, to take possession.
I straight returned, and knowing his great birth,
   Sought him accordingly in great resorts,
   In cities, theaters, gardens, parks, and courts.
At length I heard a ragged noise and mirth
   Of thieves and murderers; there I him espied,
   Who straight, "Your suit is granted," said, and died.

∽ *George Herbert*

At the round earth's imagined corners,* blow
Your trumpets, angels, and arise, arise
From death, your numberless infinities
Of souls, and to your scattered bodies go.
All whom the flood did, and fire shall o'erthrow,
All whom war, dearth, age, agues, tyrannies,
Despair, law, chance, hath slain, and you whose eyes
Shall behold God and never taste death's woe.†
But let them sleep, Lord, and me mourn a space.
For if above all these my sins abound,
'Tis late to ask abundance of Thy grace
When we are there; here on this lowly ground,
Teach me how to repent; for that's as good
As if Thou hadst sealed my pardon with Thy blood.

〜 *John Donne*

"I saw four angels standing on the four corners of the
earth." (Rev. 7:1)
† "There be some standing here, which shall not taste of
death, till they see the kingdom of God." (Luke 9:27)

Lucifer in Starlight

On a starr'd night Prince Lucifer uprose.
Tired of his dark dominion swung the fiend
   Above the rolling ball in cloud part screen'd,
Where sinners hugg'd their spectre of repose.
Poor prey to his hot fit of pride were those.
   And now upon his western wing he lean'd,
   Now his huge bulk o'er Afric's sands careen'd,
Now the black planet shadow'd Arctic snows.
Soaring through wider zones that prick'd his scars
   With memory of the old revolt from Awe,
He reach'd a middle height, and at the stars,
Which are the brain of heaven, he look'd, and sank.
Around the ancient track march'd, rank on rank,
   The army of unalterable law.

                    ∽ *George Meredith*

The Galley

My galley, charged with forgetfulness,
  Thorough sharp seas in winter nights doth pass
  'Tween rock and rock; and eke mine enemy, alas!
That is my Lord, steereth with cruelness;
And every oar a thought in readiness,
  As though that death were light in such a case.
  An endless wind doth tear the sail apace
Of forced sights* and trusty fearfulness;
A rain of tears, a cloud of dark disdain,
  Hath done the weared† cords great hinderance,
  Wreathed with error and eke with ignorance.
The stars be hid that led me to this pain.
  Drowned is reason that should me comfort,
  And I remain despairing of the port.

〜 *Sir Thomas Wyatt*

---

* sighs   † worn

The Lantern out of Doors

Sometimes a lantern moves along the night,
   That interests our eyes. And who goes there?
   I think; where from and bound, I wonder, where,
With, all down darkness wide, his wading light?

Men go by me whom either beauty bright
   In mould or mind or what not else makes rare:
   They rain against our much-thick and marsh air
Rich beams, till death or distance buys them quite.

Death or distance soon consumes them: wind
   What most I may eye after, be in at the end
I cannot, and out of sight is out of mind.

Christ minds; Christ's interest, what to avow or amend
   There, éyes them, heart wánts, care haúnts, foot
      fóllows kínd,
Their ránsom, théir rescue, ánd first, fást, last friénd.

~ *Gerard Manley Hopkins*

The Windhover:

To Christ our Lord

I caught this morning morning's minion, king-
    dom of daylight's dauphin, dapple-dawn-drawn
      Falcon, in his riding
    Of the rolling level underneath him steady air,
    and striding
High there, how he rung upon the rein of a
    wimpling wing
In his ecstasy! then off, off forth on swing,
    As a skate's heel sweeps smooth on a bow-bend:
      the hurl and gliding
    Rebuffed the big wind. My heart in hiding
Stirred for a bird,—the achieve of, the mastery
    of the thing!

Brute beauty and valour and act, oh, air, pride,
    plume, here
    Buckle! AND the fire that breaks from thee then,
    a billion
Times told lovelier, more dangerous, O my chevalier!

    No wonder of it: shéer plód makes plough down
    sillion
Shine, and blue-bleak embers, ah my dear,
    Fall, gall themselves, and gash gold-vermilion.

           ~ *Gerard Manley Hopkins*

God's Grandeur

The world is charged with the grandeur of God.
  It will flame out, like shining from shook foil;
  It gathers to a greatness, like the ooze of oil
Crushed. Why do men then now not reck his rod?
Generations have trod, have trod, have trod;
    And all is seared with trade; bleared, smeared
      with toil;
    And wears man's smudge and shares man's smell:
      the soil
Is bare now, nor can foot feel, being shod.

And for all this, nature is never spent;
  There lives the dearest freshness deep down things;
And though the last lights off the black West went
  Oh, morning, at the brown brink eastward, springs—
Because the Holy Ghost over the bent
  World broods with warm breast and with ah!
    bright wings.

～ Gerard Manley Hopkins

Sonnet

The walls surrounding them they never saw;
The angels, often. Angels were as common
As birds or butterflies, but looked more human.
As long as the wings were furled, they felt no awe.
Beasts, too, were friendly. They could find no flaw
In all of Eden: this was the first omen.
The second was the dream which woke the woman:
She dreamed she saw the lion sharpen his claw.
As for the fruit, it had no taste at all.
They had been warned of what was bound to happen;
They had been told of something called the world;
They had been told and told about the wall.
They saw it now; the gate was standing open.
As they advanced, the giant wings unfurled.

 ⌒ *Donald Justice*

Primrose

Upon a bank I sat, a child made seer
Of one small primrose flowering in my mind.
Better than wealth it is, said I, to find
One small page of Truth's manuscript made clear.
I looked at Christ transfigured without fear—
The light was very beautiful and kind,
And where the Holy Ghost in flame had signed
I read it through the lenses of a tear.
And then my sight grew dim, I could not see
The primrose that had lighted me to Heaven,
And there was but the shadow of a tree
Ghostly among the stars. The years that pass
Like tired soldiers nevermore have given
Moments to see wonders in the grass.

~ *Patrick Kavanagh*

Sonnet

You will not leave us, for You cannot, Lord.
We are the inventors of disloyalty,
And every day proclaim we dare not be
Ourselves' or Yours: at every point absurd.
For this was forged the counterfeiting word
By which the hours beguile eternity
Or cry that You are dead Who cannot die.
So in a word You are glorified and abjured.

Yet say You died and left where once You were
Nothing at all—man, beast and plant as now
In semblance, yet mere obvious nature—how
Could the blind paradox, the ridiculous
Find entrance then? What would remain with us?
Nothing, nothing at all, not even despair.

~ *Edwin Muir*

Sunday Morning

Down the road someone is practising scales,
The notes like little fishes vanish with a wink of tails,
Man's heart expands to tinker with his car
For this is Sunday morning, Fate's great bazaar;
Regard these means as ends, concentrate on this Now,
And you may grow to music or drive beyond Hindhead
    anyhow,
Take corners on two wheels until you go so fast
That you can clutch a fringe or two of the windy past,
That you can abstract this day and make it to the week
    of time
A small eternity, a sonnet self-contained in rhyme.

But listen, up the road, something gulps, the church spire
Opens its eight bells out, skulls' mouths which will
    not tire
To tell how there is no music or movement which
    secures
Escape from the weekday time. Which deadens and
    endures.

~Louis MacNeice

Sonnet 326

Weary of quests and all such poppycock
Childe Roland to the Dark Tower came once more
With a sigh that called his pilgrimage a bore,
A dull adventure, void of hope or shock.
He yawned wearily, fumbled with the lock
As he had done so many times before,
Then rapped with languid knuckles on the door
Without expecting answer to his knock.

And the world suddenly blazed and flashed and shone
With blue-green lightnings; scarlet rivers poured
Rolling floods of bright vermilion wonder:
In the riot, naked and alone,
God Almighty strode across the thunder
Roaring and brandishing a purple sword.

~ Rolfe Humphries

Once by the Pacific

The shattered water made a misty din.
Great waves looked over others coming in,
And thought of doing something to the shore
That water never did to land before.
The clouds were low and hairy in the skies,
Like locks blown forward in the gleam of eyes.
You could not tell, and yet it looked as if
The shore was lucky in being backed by cliff,
The cliff in being backed by continent;
It looked as if a night of dark intent
Was coming, and not only a night, an age.
Someone had better be prepared for rage.
There would be more than ocean-water broken
Before God's last *Put out the Light* was spoken.

⌒ Robert Frost

from Sonnets at Christmas

This is the day His hour of life draws near,
Let me get ready from head to foot for it
Most handily with eyes to pick the year
For small feed to reward a feathered wit.
Some men would see it an epiphany
At ease, at food and drink, others at chase;
Yet I, stung lassitude, with ecstasy
Unspent argue the season's difficult case
So: Man, dull creature of enormous head,
What would he look at in the coiling sky?
But I must kneel again unto the Dead
While Christmas bells of paper white and red,
Figured with boys and girls spilt from a sled,
Ring out the silence I am nourished by.

⌒Allen Tate

Barthélémon at Vauxhall

*François Hippolite Barthélémon, first-fiddler at
Vauxhall Gardens, composed what was probably the
most popular morning hymn-tune ever written. It was
formerly sung, full-voiced, every Sunday in most
churches, to Bishop Ken's words, but is now seldom
heard.*

He said: "Awake my soul, and with the sun," . . .
And paused upon the bridge, his eyes due east,
Where was emerging like a full-robed priest
The irradiate globe that vouched the dark as done.

It lit his face—the weary face of one
Who in the adjacent gardens charged his string,
Nightly, with many a tuneful tender thing,
Till stars were weak, and dancing hours outrun.

And then were threads of matin music spun
In trial tones as he pursued his way:
"This is a morn," he murmured, "well begun:
This strain to Ken will count when I am clay!"

And count it did; till, caught by echoing lyres,
It spread to galleried naves and mighty quires.

                          ∽ *Thomas Hardy*

LOVE
AND
FRIENDSHIP

"I think on thee"

To Lucia at Birth

Though the moon beaming matronly and bland
   Greets you, among the crowd of the new-born,
With "welcome to the world" yet understand
   That still her pale, lascivious unicorn
And bloody lion are loose on either hand:
   With din of bones and tantarará of horn
Their fanciful cortège parades the land—
   Pest on the high road, wild-fire in the corn.

Outrageous company to be born into,
   Lunatics of a royal age long dead.
Then reckon time by what you are or do,
   Not by the epochs of the war they spread.
   Hark how they roar; but never turn your head.
Nothing will change them, let them not change you.

            ~ *Robert Graves*

A Pair of Hands

Indeed I loved these hands and knew them well—
Nervous, expressive, holding a Chinese pink,
A child, a book always withdrawn and still
As if they had it in their power to think:
Hands that the Flemish masters have explored,
Who gave delicate strength and mystic grace
To contemplative men, to women most adored
As if to give the inmost heart a face—
Indeed I learned to love these secret hands
Before I found them here, open to mine,
And clasped the mystery no one understands,
Read reverence in their fivefold design,
Where animals and children may be healed
And in the slightest gesture Love revealed.

$\sim$ *May Sarton*

Ten-Day Leave

To my parents

House that holds me, household that I hold dear,
    Woman and man at the doorway, come what will
Hospitable—more than you know I enter here,
    In retreat, in laughter, in the need of your love still.

More perhaps than you fancy, fancy finds
    This room with books and answers in the walls;
I have continual reference to the lines
    I learned here early, later readings false.

More than you dream, I wake from a special dream
    To nothing but remorse for miles around,
And steady my bed at this unchanging scene
    When the changing dogs dispute a stranger town.

Oh, identity is a traveling-piece with some,
But here is what calls me, here what I call home.

                 ⌣ *William Meredith*

To a Troubled Friend

Weep, and weep long, but do not weep for me,
Nor, long lamenting, raise, for any word
Of mine that beats above you like a bird,
Your voice, or hand. But shaken clear, and free,
Be the bare maple, bough where nests are made
Snug in the season's wrinkled cloth of frost;
Be leaf, by hardwood knots, by tendrils crossed
On tendrils, stripped, uncaring; give no shade.

Give winter nothing; hold; and let the flake
Poise or dissolve along your upheld arms.
All flawless hexagons may melt and break;
While you must feel the summer's rage of fire,
Beyond this frigid season's empty storms,
Banished to bloom, and bear the birds' desire.

~ James Wright

In a poem made by Cummings, long since, his
Girl was the rain, but darling you are sunlight
Volleying down blue air, waking a flight
Of sighs to follow like the mourning iris
Your shining-out-of-shadow hair I miss
A fortnight and to-noon. What you excite
You are, you are me: as light's parasite
For vision on . . us. O if my syncrisis
Teases you, briefer than Propertius' in
This paraphrase by Pound—to whom I owe
Three letters—why, run through me like a comb:
I lie down flat! under your discipline
I die. No doubt of visored others, though . .
The broad sky dumb with stars shadows me home.

$\sim$ *John Berryman*

Broad on the sunburnt hill the bright moon comes,
And cuts with silver horn the hurrying cloud,
And the cold Pole Star, in the dusk, resumes
His last night's light, which light alone could shroud.
And legion other stars, that torch pursuing,
Take each their stations in the deepening night,
Lifting pale tapers for the Watch, renewing
Their glorious foreheads in the infinite.
Never before had night so many eyes.
Never was darkness so divinely thronged
As now—my love! bright star!—when you arise,
Giving me back that night which I had wronged.
Now with your voice sings all the immortal host,
This god of myriad stars whom I thought lost.

               ∽ *Conrad Aiken*

Sonnet

My thoughts through yours refracted into speech
transmute this room musically tonight,
the notes of contact flowing, rhythmic, bright
with an informal art beyond my single reach.
Outside, dark birds fly in a greening time :
wings of our sistered wishes beat these walls :
and words afflict our minds in near footfalls
approaching with a latening hour's chime.

And if an essential thing has flown between us,
rare intellectual bird of communication,
let us seize it quickly;   let our preference
choose it instead of softer things to screen us
each from the other's self : muteness or hesitation,
nor petrify live miracle by our indifference.

$\sim$ *Muriel Rukeyser*

Bread and Wine

We breakfast, walled by green, as in a bower;
Across the window-pane cloud-pictures float,
A trumpet-vine hangs there, a ruby throat
Glimmers, and is gone. Wind rocks the shaken flower.
The supper hour here is a golden hour:
Light gilds the treetops, eastward the remote
High clouds shine rosy gold, the oriole's note
Falls goldener, falling from his elm-tree tower.

Oh, in this green oasis here, we two
Together still—whatever fate provide,
To be together still! In humble pride,
I break the bread and share the wine with you,
Knowing, even as the disciples knew,
Love's very presence sitting at my side.

John Hall Wheelock

Paradox

I knew them both upon Miranda's isle,
   Which is of youth a sea-bound seigniory:
Misshapen Caliban, so seeming vile,
   And Ariel, proud prince of minstrelsy,
Who did forsake the sunset for my tower
   And like a star above my slumber burned.
The night was held in silver chains by power
   Of melody, in which all longings yearned—
Star-grasping youth in one wild strain expressed,
   Tender as dawn, insistent as the tide;
The heart of night and summer stood confessed.
   I rose aglow and flung the lattice wide—
Ah jest of art, what mockery and pang!
   Alack, it was poor Caliban who sang.

⁓ *Willa Cather*

The Favorite

A knave who scampered through the needle's eye,
He never trembled at a veiled remark.
His oyster world was easily come by;
There were no nights of sleeping in the park.

Fearless and bold, he did his fellows in,
Only to gain fresh triumphs and applause.
His insolence could wear no patience thin.
He lived beyond the touch of mortal laws.

O he was Fortune's child, a favorite son
Upon whom every gift and thrill were showered,
And yet his happiness was not complete;
Slowly his matchless disposition soured
Until he cried at enemies undone
And longed to feel the impact of defeat.

⌣ Theodore Roethke

"Vien dietro a me a lascia dir le genti."—DANTE
"Contando i casi della vita nostra."—PETRARCA

Many in aftertimes will say of you
    "He loved her"—while of me what will they say?
    Not that I loved you more than just in play,
For fashion's sake as idle women do.
Even let them prate; who know not what we knew
    Of love and parting in exceeding pain,
    Of parting hopeless here to meet again,
Hopeless on earth, and heaven is out of view.
But by my heart of love laid bare to you,
    My love that you can make not void nor vain,
Love that foregoes you but to claim anew
Beyond this passage of the gate of death,
    I charge you at the Judgment make it plain
My love of you was life and not a breath.

                  ∽ *Christina Rossetti*

Loving in truth, and fain in verse my love to show,
That she, dear she, might take some pleasure of my
pain,
Pleasure might cause her read, reading might make
her know,
Knowledge might pity win, and pity grace obtain,—
I sought fit words to paint the blackest face to woe;
Studying inventions fine, her wits to entertain,
Oft turning others' leaves to see if thence would flow
Some fresh and fruitful showers upon my sun-burned
brain.
But words came halting forth, wanting invention's stay;
Invention, nature's child, fled step-dame Study's
blows,
And others' feet still seemed but strangers in my
way.
Thus, great with child to speak, and helpless in my
throes,
Biting my truant pen, beating myself for spite,
Fool, said my muse to me, look in thy heart and
write.

~ *Sir Philip Sidney*

I lived with Dreams for all my company
Instead of men & women, years ago,
And found them gentle mates, nor thought to know
A sweeter music than they played to me.
But soon their trailing purple was not free
Of this world's dust; their lutes did silent grow,
And I myself grew faint and blind below
Their vanishing eyes. Then *thou* didst come . . . to be,
Beloved, what they *seemed*. Their shining fronts,
Their songs, their splendours, . . . (better, yet the
    same, . .
As river-water hallowed into fonts . . .)
Met in thee, and, from out thee, overcame
My soul with satisfaction of all wants—
Because God's gifts put man's best dreams to shame.

                Elizabeth Barrett Browning

"His wife not dead a month—and there he sits,
Heartless and doubtless happy": so they said
Who at the game between the Gold and Red
Remarked me.—   Meantime bases, bats, and mitts,
Pitchers and fielders, flags and fouls and hits
(When up the sky careered the shining ball),
The runners diving in the dust, and all,
Made one blurred nightmare.   By my sober wits,
'Twas "most indecorous" that there I sat,
My wife not dead a month!—   Did I not know
The use of crepe, the etiquette of woe?—
Yes; but I'd business more severe than that:
Knowing how hungrily Death leered for me,
I seized on life wherever it might be.

∽ *William Ellery Leonard*

This poem is part of a sonnet series entitled "Two Lives"
which tells the story of a tragic marriage. Some of the
most famous series are those of Shakespeare, Donne,
and Wordsworth.—H.P.

Like as, to make our appetites more keen,
With eager compounds we our palate urge;
As, to prevent our maladies unseen,
We sicken to shun sickness when we purge;
Even so, being full of your ne'er-cloying sweetness,
To bitter sauces did I frame my feeding;
And sick of welfare found a kind of meetness
To be diseased, ere that there was true needing.
Thus policy in love, to anticipate
The ills that were not, grew to faults assured,
And brought to medicine a healthful state,
Which, rank of goodness, would by ill be cured:
But thence I learn, and find the lesson true,
Drugs poison him that so fell sick of you.

᷍ *William Shakespeare*

Since there's no help, come let us kiss and part;
Nay, I have done, you get no more of me,
And I am glad, yea glad with all my heart
That thus so cleanly I myself can free;
Shake hands forever, cancel all our vows,
And when we meet at any time again,
Be it not seen in either of our brows
That we one jot of former love retain.
Now at the last gasp of love's latest breath,
When, his pulse failing, passion speechless lies,
When faith is kneeling by his bed of death,
And innocence is closing up his eyes,
    Now if thou wouldst, when all have given him over,
    From death to life thou mightst him yet recover.

∽ Michael Drayton

Waiting

What reasons may the single heart employ
When, forward and impervious, it moves
Through savage times and science toward the joy
Of love's next meeting in a threatened space?
What privilege is this, whose tenure gives
One anesthetic hour of release,
While the air raid's spattered signature displays
A bitter artistry among the trees?

Thus, in our published era, sweetness lives
And keeps its reasons in a private room:
As, in the hothouse, white hibiscus proves
A gardener's thesis all the winter through,
So does this tenderness of waiting bloom
Like tropics under glass, my dear, for you.

~ *John Malcolm Brinnin*

The Wakening

Looking up at last from the first sleep
Of necessity rather than of pure delight
While his dreams still rode and lapped like the morning
    light
That everywhere in the world shimmered and lay deep

So that his sight was half dimmed with its dazzling,
    he could see
Her standing naked in the day-shallows there,
Face turned away, hands lost in her bright hair;
And he saw then that her shadow was the tree:

For in a place where he could never come
Only its darkness underlay the day's splendour,
So that even as she stood there it must reach down

Through not roots but branches with dark bird-song,
    into a stream
Of silence like a sky but deeper
Than this light or than any remembered heaven.

                            W. S. Merwin

Imitation

Let men take note of her, touching her shyness,
How grace informs and presses the brocade
Wherein her benefits are whitely stayed,
And think all glittering enterprise, and highness
Of blood or deed were yet in something minus
Lacking the wide approval of her mouth,
And to betoken every man his drouth,
Drink, in her name, all tankards to their dryness.

Wanting her clear perfection, how may tongues
Manifest what no language understands?
Yet as her beauty evermore commands
Even the tanager with tiny lungs
To flush all silence, may she by these songs
Know it was love I looked for at her hands.

∼ Anthony Hecht

When in the chronicle of wasted time
I see descriptions of the fairest wights,
And beauty making beautiful old rhyme
In praise of ladies dead and lovely knights;
Then, in the blazon of sweet beauty's best,
Of hand, of foot, of lip, of eye, of brow,
I see their antique pen would have expressed
Even such a beauty as you master now.
So all their praises are but prophecies
Of this our time, all you prefiguring,
And, for they looked but with divining eyes,
They had not still enough your worth to sing:
    For we, which now behold these present days,
    Have eyes to wonder, but lack tongues to praise.

                        William Shakespeare

Then hate me when thou wilt; if ever, now;
Now, while the world is bent my deeds to cross,
Join with the spite of fortune, make me bow,
And do not drop in for an after-loss.
Ah, do not, when my heart hath 'scaped this sorrow,
Come in the rearward of a conquered woe;
Give not a windy night a rainy morrow,
To linger out a purposed overthrow.
If thou wilt leave me, do not leave me last,
When other petty griefs have done their spite,
But in the onset come; so shall I taste
At first the very worst of fortune's might,
    And other strains of woe, which now seem woe,
    Compared with loss of thee will not seem so.

〜 William Shakespeare

117

What potions have I drunk of Siren tears
Distilled from limbecks foul as hell within,
Applying fears to hopes and hopes to fears,
Still losing when I saw myself to win!
What wretched errors hath my heart committed,
Whilst it hath thought itself so blessed never!
How have mine eyes out of their spheres been fitted
In the distraction of this madding fever!
O, benefit of ill: now I find true
That better is by evil still made better;
And ruined love, when it is built anew,
Grows fairer than at first, more strong, far greater.
  So I return rebuked to my content,
  And gain by ills thrice more than I have spent.

~ *William Shakespeare*

118

TIME
"Devouring Time"

Devouring Time, blunt thou the lion's paws,
And make the earth devour her own sweet brood.
Pluck the keen teeth from the fierce tiger's jaws,
And burn the long-lived phoenix in her blood.
Make glad and sorry seasons as thou fleet'st,
And do whate'er thou wilt, swift-footed Time,
To the wide world and all her fading sweets,
But I forbid thee one most heinous crime.
Oh, carve not with thy hours my love's fair brow,
Nor draw no lines there with thine antique pen.
Him in thy course untainted do allow
For beauty's pattern to succeeding men.

    Yet do thy worst, old Time. Despite thy wrong,
    My love shall in my verse ever live young.

                    ~ *William Shakespeare*

Piazza Piece

—I am a gentleman in a dustcoat trying
To make you hear. Your ears are soft and small
And listen to an old man not at all,
They want the young men's whispering and sighing.
But see the roses on your trellis dying
And hear the spectral singing of the moon;
For I must have my lovely lady soon,
I am a gentleman in a dustcoat trying.

—I am a lady young in beauty waiting
Until my truelove comes, and then we kiss.
But what grey man among the vines is this
Whose words are dry and faint as in a dream?
Back from my trellis, Sir, before I scream!
I am a lady young in beauty waiting.

∼ *John Crowe Ransome*

The Road

The great road stretched before them, clear and still,
Then from in front one cried: "Turn back! Turn back!"
Yet they had never seen so fine a track,
Honest and frank past any thought of ill.
But when they glanced behind, how strange, how
    strange,
These wild demented windings in and out—
Traced by some devil of mischief or of doubt?—
That was the road they had come by. Could it change?

How could they penetrate that perilous maze
Backwards, again, climb backwards down the scree
From the wrong side, slither among the dead?
Yet as they travelled on, for many days
These words rang in their ears as if they said,
"There was another road you did not see."

                   Edwin Muir

To the Greatest City in the World

No permanent possession of the sky
Nor everlasting lease upon the air
Is given any town. *Prepare, prepare
To see your towers falling.* By and by,
Vertical city, delicate and high,
Even your cliffs must crack, topple, and share
The common doom that blunter buildings bear,
Tumble and crumble, disappear and die.

And some day solemn folk, who never knew
Except from ancient hearsay, all your wonder
Of splendid elevating steel and stones
Will come with shovels, rummaging for you,
With dredges pull the river mud from under
Your rusting huddled fragmentary bones.

⌐ *Rolfe Humphries*

This is my play's last scene, here heavens appoint
My pilgrimage's last mile; and my race,
Idly yet quickly run, hath this last pace,
My span's last inch, my minute's last point,
And gluttonous death will instantly unjoint
My body and soul, and I shall sleep a space,
But my ever-waking part shall see that face
Whose fear already shakes my every joint:
Then, as my soul to heaven, her first seat, takes flight,
And earth-born body in the earth shall dwell,
So, fall my sins, that all may have their right,
To where they're bred, and would press me, to hell.
Impute me righteous, thus purged of evil,
For thus I leave the world, the flesh, the devil.

∽ *John Donne*

Since brass, nor stone, nor earth, nor boundless sea,
But sad mortality o'er-sways their power,
How with this rage shall beauty hold a plea
Whose action is no stronger than a flower?
O, how shall summer's honey breath hold out
Against the wreckful siege of battering days,
When rocks impregnable are not so stout,
Nor gates of steel so strong, but Time decays?
O fearful meditation! where, alack,
Shall Time's best jewel from Time's chest lie hid?
Or what strong hand can hold his swift foot back?
Or who his spoil of beauty can forbid?
    O, none, unless this miracle have might,
    That in black ink my love may still shine bright.

~ *William Shakespeare*

Remembered Gaiety

Remembered gaiety hurts mind and heart
As present pain is impotent to do.
The moment's loss, courageously lived through,
Can die; but not those sudden days that start
And breathe again, immortally apart
From earlier, from after. They are few,
And chance's children; yet their smiles renew
More sadness than death does with all his art.

The people in this picture think to stand
On this same rock forever; he that waves,
And she that simpers—underneath what sun
Do they lie now, forgetting? Wind and sand
That blow here since—O, tell me why time saves,
Merciless, one moment, only one?

∽ Mark Van Doren

Not from the stars do I my judgment pluck;
And yet methinks I have astronomy,
But not to tell of good or evil luck,
Of plagues, of dearths, or season's quality;
Nor can I fortune to brief minutes tell,
Pointing to each his thunder, rain and wind,
Or say with princes if it shall go well,
By oft predict that I in heaven find:
But from thine eyes my knowledge I derive,
And, constant stars, in them I read such art,
As truth and beauty shall together thrive,
If from thyself to store thou wouldst convert;
    Or else of thee this I prognosticate:
    Thy end is truth's and beauty's doom and date.

⁓ William Shakespeare

The House in Bonac Revisited

I am in love with the impossible:
From the beginning, I have tried to bring
Into the toils of language the fierce thing
No word may gather and no tongue may tell—
And it was in this room that first the spell
Was cast upon me for a curse, to wring
My heart in labor and in suffering,
Under these rafters that I love so well.

How many a night, how many a lonely year,
With mind grown bitter and with blood gone dry,
I have wrought these cunning toils! Nevertheless,
All longing was repaid, all bitterness,
In moments when my heart stood still to hear,
Even for a moment, that fleet foot go by.

~ John Hall Wheelock

Simple Autumnal

The measured blood beats out the year's delay.
The tearless eyes and heart, forbidden grief,
Watch the burned, restless, but abiding leaf,
The brighter branches arming the bright day.

The cone, the curving fruit should fall away,
The vine stem crumble, ripe grain know its sheaf.
Bonded to time, fires should have done, be brief,
But, serfs to sleep, they glitter and they stay.

Because not last nor first, grief in its prime
Wakes in the day, and hears of life's intent.
Sorrow would break the seal stamped over time
And set the baskets where the bough is bent.

Full season's come, yet filled trees keep the sky
And never scent the ground where they must lie.

~ *Louise Bogan*

The Reunion

I loved the apple-sweetness of the air
And pines that settled slanting on the hill,
Indians old and soft with needles there,
Where once we stood, and both so strangely still.
We must have surely known what other days
Would come in other flaming autumn's flame.
And even though we walk through different ways
To different hills that hill remains the same.
Watch every splendor, envy all the sky,
But recognize the days we knew, and hear
The simple sounds we heard. As birds that fly
Southward to warmth, we shall come back one year.
The little teeth of time will make no mark
On any stone, on any leaf or bark.

༄ *Owen Dodson*

No, Time, thou shalt not boast that I do change.
Thy pyramids built up with newer might
To me are nothing novel, nothing strange;
They are but dressings of a former sight.
Our dates are brief, and therefore we admire
What thou dost foist upon us that is old,
And rather make them born to our desire
Than think that we before have heard them told.
Thy registers and thee I both defy,
Not wond'ring at the present, nor the past;
For thy records and what we see doth lie,
Made more or less by thy continual haste.
　　This I do vow, and this shall ever be:
　　I will be true despite thy scythe and thee.

〜 *William Shakespeare*

Weary with toil, I haste me to my bed,
The dear repose for limbs with travel tired,
But then begins a journey in my head
To work my mind when body's work's expired;
For then my thoughts, from far where I abide,
Intend a zealous pilgrimage to thee,
And keep my drooping eyelids open wide,
Looking on darkness which the blind do see;
Save that my soul's imaginary sight
Presents thy shadow to my sightless view,
Which like a jewel hung in ghastly night,
Makes black night beauteous and her old face new.
  Lo, thus, by day my limbs, by night my mind,
  For thee, and for myself, no quiet find.

             ❧ *William Shakespeare*

Come, sleep, O sleep, the certain knot of peace,
   The baiting place of wit, the balm of woe,
The poor man's wealth, the prisoner's release,
   Th' indifferent judge between the high and low;
With shield of proof shield me from out the prease *
   Of those fierce darts despair at me doth throw;
O make me in those civil wars to cease;
   I will good tribute pay, if thou do so.
Take thou of me smooth pillows, sweetest bed,
   A chamber deaf to noise and blind to light,
A rosy garland and a weary head;
   And if these things, as being thine by right,
      Move not thy heavy grace, thou shalt in me,
      Livelier than elsewhere, Stella's image see.

⌒ *Sir Philip Sidney*

---

* crowd

With Garb of Proof

". . . with garb of proof shield me from out the prease/
Of those fierce darts Despair at me doth throw"/
                                    —Sir Philip Sidney

"With garb of proof"—but where, in our time, find
Armor invisible, chain-mail for the heart
Against all flight of evil, each fierce dart
Tipped with peculiar poison, in a wind
Implacable, incessant, and combined
With sleet-sting, gnat-bite? What surpassing art
Can stop, break, turn, that arrow fire, or part
That cloud of menace-motes around the mind?

Ah, good Sir Philip, as you must have known,
That was no light demand you laid on Sleep
As officer, but I would wish my own
More vigilant, my watch and ward to keep,
Alert, responsible, a sentinel
More open-eyed, to guard, and wish me well.

                              ⁓ *Rolfe Humphries*

Death be not proud, though some have called thee
Mighty and dreadful, for thou art not so;
For those whom thou think'st thou dost overthrow
Die not, poor death, nor yet canst thou kill me.
From rest and sleep, which but thy pictures be,
Much pleasure; then from thee much more must flow,
And soonest our best men with thee do go,
Rest of their bones, and soul's delivery.*
Thou art slave to fate, chance, kings, and desperate
      men,
And dost with poison, war, and sickness dwell;
And poppy or charms can make us sleep as well,
And better than thy stroke; why swell'st thou then?
One short sleep past, we wake eternally,
And death shall be no more; death, thou shalt die.

$\smallsmile$ *John Donne*

---

* Rescue, deliverance; also, the bringing forth or "birth"
of the soul

A Prayer to Time

Time, that anticipates eternities
And has an art to resurrect the rose;
Time, whose lost siren song at evening blows
With sun-flushed cloud shoreward on toppling seas;
Time, arched by planets lonely in the vast
Sadness that darkens with the fall of day;
Time, unexplored elysium; and the grey
Death-shadow'd pyramid that we name the past—
    Magnanimous Time, patient with man's vain glory;
    Ambition's road; Lethe's awaited guest;
    Time, hearkener to the stumbling passionate story
    Of human failure humanly confessed;
    Time, on whose stair we dream our hopes of heaven,
    Help us to judge ourselves, and so be shriven.

~ Siegfried Sassoon

The First Seven Years

That was a time of furniture and family
and books and gramophones and happiness
and afternoon and servants and late tea
and lamps, my mother in a trailing dress,
the vases on the mantel white and blue,
the cat asleep along the window sill.
Our Victor with the morning-glory horn
held Farrar and Caruso in its walnut case
and bugled Marguerites and Butterflies.
The rainbow fairy books by Andrew Lang
with Eisenkopf and princesses forlorn
displayed their simple magics to my face.
The antiques of the heart can spell me still.
That wood was haunted and the bluebird sang.

～ *Richmond Lattimore*

The Sacrament

Once again, good silver and crystal,
a centerpiece of plastic flowers, and linen
from the cedar chest arranged with skill.
With whispered grace we let the year begin.

The tree yet hung, the windows sprayed with snow,
the mantel lined with bottles of empty wine.
A lamp sheds paper mistletoe.
With whispered grace we let the year begin.

The fire of pressed logs, pale as tinsel,
flickers on the turkey's basted skin.
We'd like to find some way to win
the past year, some religious flame to fill

its hide with more than aging flesh and bone.
With whispered grace we enter time again.

⌒ William Heyen

139

The Snow Globe

A long time ago, when I was a child,
They left my light on while I went to sleep,
As though they would have wanted me beguiled
By brightness if at all; dark was too deep.

And they left me one toy, a village white
With the fresh snow and silently in glass
Frozen forever. But if you shook it,
The snow would rise up in the rounded space

And from the limits of the universe
Snow itself down again. O world of white,
First home of dreams! Now that I have my dead,
I want so cold an emblem to rehearse
How many of them have gone from the world's light,
As I have gone, too, from my snowy bed.

$\sim$ *Howard Nemerov*

Sic Transit

Sometimes I wake and hear far in the night
The clip-clop of an old horse down the street
And bless the measured music of his feet,
The way he moves without his tail alight,
His eyes a-glare, and noises in his nose,
How slowly and at honorable pace
Drawing his ash-cart, decently he goes—
As fits the remnant of a splendid race.

My grandson's grandson somewhere in the rack
Of time will wake one night, and hear below
The levels where the winking air-lines glow
A rumble like a beetle on its back,
And smile, and bless the last old motor car
Rattling to join the horse and dinosaur.

꩜ *Nancy Byrd Turner*

141

O Earth, unhappy planet born to die,
Might I your scribe and your confessor be,
What wonders must you not relate to me
Of Man, who when his destiny was high
Strode like the sun into the middle sky
And shone an hour, and who so bright as he,
And like the sun went down into the sea,
Leaving no spark to be remembered by.
But no; you have not learned in all these years
To tell the leopard and the newt apart;
Man, with his singular laughter, his droll tears,
His engines and his conscience and his art,
Made but a simple sound upon your ears:
The patient beating of the animal heart.

            ∽ *Edna St. Vincent Millay*

INDEXES

Index to Authors

Index to Titles

Index to First Lines

Acknowledgments

Permission to reprint copyrighted poems is gratefully acknowledged to the following:

Atheneum Publishers, Inc., for "Imitation" from *The Hard Hours* by Anthony Hecht, Copyright 1954, © 1967 by Anthony E. Hecht; "Memo to Gongora" from *Daylight Saving* by Daryl Hine, Copyright © 1978 by Daryl Hine; "The Wakening" from *The First Four Books of Poems* by W. S. Merwin (originally published in *Green with Beasts*), Copyright © 1955, 1956, 1975 by W. S. Merwin; and "Modified Sonnets" from *A Swim off the Rocks* by Howard Moss, Copyright ©1976 by Howard Moss.

Brandt & Brandt Literary Agency, Inc., for "The Trapeze Performer" by Stephen Vincent Benet from *The Selected Works of Stephen Vincent Benet*, Copyright, 1942 by Stephen Vincent Benet, Copyright renewed ©, 1966 by Thomas C. Benet, Stephanie B. Mahin & Rachel Benet Lewis.

John Malcolm Brinnin, for "Waiting" from *The Selected Poems of John Malcolm Brinnin*.

Curtis Brown, Ltd., for "To Lucia at Birth" from *Poems 1935–1945* by Robert Graves, Copyright © 1945 by Robert Graves.

Chatto and Windus Ltd. (for Canada), for "Burden" from *Collected Poems 1930–1976* by Richard Eberhart.

Wm. Collins Sons & Co., Ltd. (for Canada), for "The Genuine Article" from *Poems* by C. S. Lewis.

The Devin-Adair Co., Old Greenwich, Conn. 06870, for "Primrose" from *Collected Poems* by Patrick Kavanagh, Copyright © 1964 by The Devin-Adair Co.

Dodd, Mead & Company, Inc., for "Sic Transit" from *Star in a Well* by Nancy Byrd Turner, Copyright 1935 by Dodd, Mead & Company, Inc., Copyright renewed 1963 by Nancy Byrd Turner.

Doubleday & Company, Inc., for "Sonnet" from *A Star by Day* by David McCord, Copyright 1950 by David McCord; and "The Favorite," Copyright 1941 by Theodore Roethke, from *The Collected Poems of Theodore Roethke*.

E. P. Dutton, for "August Nostalgia" from *Collected Poems* by Louise Townsend Nicholl, Copyright 1953 by E. P. Dutton & Co., Inc.

Norma Millay (Ellis), Literary Executor, for "To Inez Milholland" and sonnet beginning "O Earth, unhappy planet born to die" from *Collected Poems* by Edna St. Vincent Millay, Harper & Row, Copyright 1934, 1941, 1962, 1968.

Faber and Faber Ltd. (for Canadian permission), for "A Misunderstanding" and "Who's Who" from *Collected Poems* by W. H. Auden; "Sunday Morning" from *The Collected Poems of Louis MacNeice*; and "Sonnet" and "The Road" from *Collected Poems of Edwin Muir*.

Farrar, Straus & Giroux, Inc., for "In a poem made by Cummings" and "Marble nor monuments" from *Berryman's Sonnets* by John Berryman, Copyright © 1952, 1967 by John Berryman; "Some Dreams They Forgot" from *The Complete Poems* by Elizabeth Bishop, Copyright 1933, © 1966 by Elizabeth Bishop; "Simple Autumnal" and "Single Sonnet" from *The Blue Estuaries* by Louise Bogan, Copyright © 1927, 1936, 1968 by Louise Bogan, Copyright renewed © 1953 by Louise Bogan; "Jeremiah" from *Light Verse and Satires* by Witter Bynner, Copyright © 1977,

j821.04
T
Plo

This powerful
rhyme

DATE			
	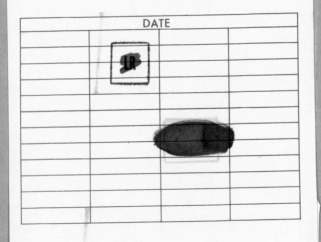		

89-9096
821.04
Plo